T0345536

The Nomads, My Brothers,
Go Out to Drink from the Big Dipper

THE AFRICA LIST

The Nomads, My Brothers,
Go Out to Drink from the Big Dipper

ABDOURAHMAN A. WABERI

TRANSLATED BY NANCY NAOMI CARLSON

LONDON NEW YORK CALCUTTA

This project was supported in part by a literature translation fellowship from the National Endowment for the Arts.

National Endowment for the Arts
arts.gov

ART WORKS.

This work is published via the Publication Assistance Programme Tagore, with the support of Institut Français en Inde / Ambassade de France en Inde and the Institut Français de Paris

Seagull Books, 2015

Originally published as *Les nomades, mes frères, vont boire à la grande ourse* © Abdourahman A. Waberi, 2013

Published by arrangement with Agence litteraire Pierre Astier & Associés

English translation © Nancy Naomi Carlson, 2015

ISBN 978 0 8574 2 238 5

British Cataloguing-in-Publication Data

A catalogue record for this book is available from the British Library

Typeset by Seagull Books, Calcutta, India

Printed and bound by Maple Press, York, Pennsylvania

For Osman, Toronto's lone sun
In memory of the writer Abdi Ismaël Abdi
too soon departed

TABLE OF CONTENTS

ACKNOWLEDGEMENTS

Asymptote: 'Ai-yai-yai', 'The Elixir of Exile', 'Here Is', 'Sketch II'

Beltway Poetry Quarterly: 'Acacia', 'Brief Discourse in the Style of Edmond Jabès', 'White Thread Black Thread', 'Yesterday's Tales'

Boulevard: 'Infancy'

The Broadkill Review: 'Caress', 'Coral Riffs', 'Eight Faces', 'Grieving Dawn', 'Ink Drawings', 'Landmark', 'Night Collage'

Cider Press Review: 'A Sky Chart'

Colorado Review: 'Untitled Canvas'

Connotation Press: An Online Artifact: 'Japanese Cherry Tree', 'Predawn', 'Wind is a Calligrapher'

Drunken Boat: 'By Night', 'Engravings', 'Time'

Hampden-Sydney Poetry Review: 'Equipment', 'Lament of the Lame Herdsman', 'There'

Hayden's Ferry Review: 'After the Rain', 'Caravan of Words'

Notre Dame Review: 'Acacia', 'Elegy for a Fly', 'Yesterday's Tales'

Ozone Park Journal: 'Anatomy (She-camel)', 'Bilal', 'Dharma', and 'Shattered Vision'

Poetry International: 'Untitled'

Prairie Schooner: 'Nomadic Miniatures'

Taos Journal of Poetry & Art: 'Canvas with Ochre and Foam', 'Ouabain'

Tupelo Quarterly: 'Sketch I'

Weave: 'Desires'

West Branch: 'Brief Discourse in the Style of Edmond Jabès', 'Truce'

THE WAY OF SIMPLICITY

From all our combined machinery, from all our roads
mapped out in miles, from all the tonnage we've amassed,
from all our aircrafts placed side by side,
from our rules, our conditioning,
not even the slightest emotion could emerge . . .
True civilized worlds are poetic shocks:
shock of stars, sun, plants,
animals, shock of the round globe,
of rain, light, numbers,
shock of life, shock of death . . .
Civilization's true manifestation is myth . . .
In the current state of affairs, the only avowed
haven of the mythic spirit is poetry.
And poetry is a rebellion against society—
devotion to myth, abandoned or exiled or razed . . .
Alone the poetic spirit corrodes and constructs, refines and revives.

Aimé Césaire, *Calling the Magician*
May 1944, Haiti

Often beyond my awareness, the horizon leads me back, shining there, at the very end of stretches of land in movement, in levitation, melting and becoming like aether before our bewildered eyes. In search of shade, the gaze turns away from matter in fusion, but admires the evening star before ricocheting back to earth:

loose stones entangled with piles of sand, stalks of grass and touches of green vegetation adorning the austere and foreboding landscape.

It is here, we all know, where man stood upright for the first time. Here, in this region, where mankind put one foot in front of the other. *Homo erectus*, free and walking. The act of movement, the origin of gesture, takes root in breath. I try to grasp that instant's past, present and future at the same time. I love to imagine that man made his first gestures in the bed of my pages. And if readers are able to experience the shadow of that impression while reading this collection, I will be happy and refreshed by the breath of their presence. A balm for my heart and a sharing. A banquet of words. My head, skin, all of my body would be energized by the act of reading, this form of miraculous meeting. And there I will be again, in the breath of the instant, now on the verge of vertigo, now still and silent like the ibis of ancient times.

I remain attracted to the desert, its silence, its vastness and its burning wind. The desert of my nomadic ancestors is not a tourist attraction. My brothers, the nomads, only set forth out of necessity, always following paths that have withstood the test of time. Often reluctantly. Always wisely. They combine movement and rootedness, not leaving markers to find their way back, nor unearthing buried treasure. No, the issue is much more serious—a question of life or death. If they move again, it is to escape the slipknot of hunger. To get rid of all fat, all superfluous and useless things. A heart quick to assist, a hint of disbelief in the corner of the lips, all one needs is to fly like an eagle with no worries of clocks nor hourglasses. To walk, to migrate with family and herds, is not a luxury but an economic necessity. Better yet, an ecological wisdom.

These little poems come from the past, with some as old as twenty years and some a mere few weeks. Most of them were written between 1991 and 1998, and are joined by their young brothers, composed recently (poems for Timbuktu). To write poetry is a matter of the strictest necessity. I frugally sow these modest pebbles. In truth, 'sow' is too grandiose a description, as it would be more accurate to say these poems come to me when they want. Sprung from God knows where, they seem to follow their own maturity cycle. Discreetly, perhaps secretly willing to keep their distance from the fashionable mills of words where talkative hordes congregate, brewing batches of goods. These words remain alert. They sometimes happen to vanish by way of modesty or habit. None get lost in the desert of the page.

These poems tend to avoid excess—what philosophers of ancient times called hubris—which is the character of today's world. Economical, financial, environmental excess all over the globe, even in the poorest countries. Also personal excess which blinds individuals, throwing them into meaningless consumption. Another path of life is possible, apparent in the creases and folds of this collection. Simplicity, the joy of living, the refusal of excess and idle talk, therein lies the way. And thus the mindful acceptance of all our emotions is accessible to all of us. Follow the gaze of poets and watch for their feet powdered by the dust of wandering. They will invite you to taste happy simplicity. They will help you, hopefully, to make yourself the master of your own way of living, for an hour or an eternity.

Abdourahman A. Waberi

ENGRAVINGS

1

between rubble and sovereign sun
all water consumed
all wailing subdued
since dawn
time
this land remains the same:
the open wound of Africa

2

a tortured geology
seen by the bird as it soars
beneath each step
skin stripped clean
no clouds of ash
not yet

3

Ardoukoba☆
is proud
since awakening men
were they too stone-faced
to suit his taste?

4

that the Prophet had to bless the land of the Habash[☆]—
in remembrance of Bilal^{☆☆}—
does not explain my afflicted shore

5

the herd is thinner here
than anywhere else
anyway so are the men

6

a port
a town
garrison
a simple railroad track
a fortress considered rich
in one's own backyard

7

for miniature republic
parsimonious poems

CARAVAN OF WORDS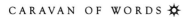

Here Is

where you hear the vibrato of Oum Kalthoum*
where you harbour doubts about the Good Lord
and faceless neighbours
and where you'll swear to me to have heard the ghost
of the happy traveller
while waiting to drown your distress
in glasses
the colour of pus

Litany

1

The eternal chant of the Word for its life
in the sky of the ages
I hear the wilds of childhood
memory's wise calligraphies
imprinted in the split second's spit
I also hear chains of words from a distant past
pieces of flesh
vocal carrion
following secret routes
of graveyards turned to dust
literality bares ancestral fears
that none can dispute
I hear the human voice of the wadi
where they replay the old rivalry
of narrator and writer who loses faith
I hear the hail of words like so many lianes
that drop from a sky without cage

2

the tree of knowledge has wings to surpass the horizon

3

to steal the verb
behind the back of the guard who caresses the patina of days

4

we'll have to make room for the banished 'p' ☆
that slips back like a plaintive spouse
on tippytoes into her house

Wind Is a Calligrapher

brush in hand the wind sketches
landscapes of words
sculpted mountain slopes
shadow plains
horizon enclaves

the calligrapher tickles
desert furrows of fire
with quite a delicate stroke of ink

Equipment

let nomadic words live—
muslin damask
cashmere gazelle alcove☆
sari banana alcohol meringue . . .—
colony soft as silk
azure to touch

cottons outlining bones
oral ancestors' shadow
resisting harsh winters
deployed by the prism
silhouette of the past

Ouabain ☆

I open the dictionary, read
in French: 'n.f. (1892; from Somali *ouabaïo*).
Medicine. One of the cardiotonic glucosides . . .
extracted from seeds of the glabrous strophanthus shrub.'
This is Somali's only clear contribution
to French

Miniatures

> *There are those who are born of the sun*
> *Who, by their lips, give life to the withered leaf*
> Mazisi Kunene☆

1

Day Full of Light

night dreamily nude
swallowed stars
day's catapult
waits for the sun to turn
the barren sea carmine

we live at the sun's threshold
you don't believe me?
come inspect my home
if you'd like

colours of day
rise again from the well
(night)
hate descends to threaten the tribe

spiralling notes of the muezzin
(cowhand of dawn)
have just given a sign to the stars
as they die

2

Bohemian Themes for Nomadic Poems

the poet is dying here in this world
he only survives in the bosom of memory
amassing a small store of works
fine watercolour art
parcels of life

we wrestle with life
to make it worthwhile
why just blame our rebellious youth?
to milk of day
I prefer ink of night

humanity is a network
and what about this great sky
colour of earth?

Brief Discourse in the Style of Edmond Jabès ☆

my tree the aloe
my flower the crack in the cactus
my river none in my land
my universe desert basalt
my entourage camelids
my weapon the dagger's blade
my shadow is rangy
survival is my life's work
essential
my landscape the changeless horizon
the dust stirred up
by sheepskin soles
the territory still
before me
my guide the desert
my text the sky
each evening regained
my word each stone
each flint
my dream always the same:

nomad fathered

in economy most austere . . .

INK DRAWINGS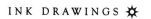

1

the portrait presents a condensed view
of the body's landscape
Cyclops' lamp-eye begins to set time
the world closes in on the face's ring
portraits aren't the photographer's business

2

eye-opener☆ hiding its pain
pushes on like the jackal
to pluck the horizon
eye-opener reveals with equal zeal
the entrails of night and parchment of day
starfish flout the sun at noon
the poem tries to hold again
the backwash of spoken words

3

I'll hope for a necklace of echoes
by way of a gift
nourishment of eyes
shifting scenes
sands the colour of gold
rampart of angry tides
changeable moons seeking a matchless shade

4

fatal glare of the white page
saliva
poisoned index finger
death arranges a date—
flesh and old bones—
no name for the rose for a thousand nights
fatal glare of the white page

Sketch I

I'm the one who intones: 'I'm never alone'
I chat with my drafts, shade in spaces
invent little tales
like the one of that family whose pose
is awkward
caught by the studio camera's lens

Sketch II

repetition affirms identity
by seizing again
and not by imposing a rainbow
(that necktie of cosmic wedded bliss)
equally fleeting as fair

Canvas with Ochre and Foam

entry to self
invisible canal
exit toward others
nature is turning corrosive
at our feet the cactus drops violets
gone mad

Night Collage

African ancient face
another man's face
face of a female child
waiting room
orange sky
dancers from back
dancers full-face
little girl in tears
chilli pepper crushed
young man bearing a wheelbarrow
woman-moon who weaves
infant who sucks
sun setting on village dawn
man talking to self
and sees walking woman lace
chicken for sacrifice
solar pump
woman rocks baby and goatskin bag
people and places slowly connect
and melt

Untitled Canvas

country of others
another country
different country that laughs at me

another myself whispers to pick
for my own kingdom the white page
and wander through life

we are that sheep of Panurge☆
bracing ourselves
on the grey verge of no man's land

the Somali bullet: bloom of a new genus
that bans
all transports of joy
all shedding of tears in the name of love
drawn from the bittersweet milk of peace

Time

the foam of daydreams dissolving
when brushed by the raw real world
never stops bubbling before my eyes
I see it now as I see you
in this gaping day of post-night

everything floats enclosed in its form-to-be

the seed claims to push a stalk, weak
as a phallus post-sex
trapped between being and time

Predawn

half-certainty of island dawn
that strange moment which falls in the earliest hours
while waiting for morning to gather strength

as this genesis starts
boys shiver in *qamis*✶ of wool
a baby nuzzles her mother's neck
like a spider who starts
against her will
the race toward death

EVERY DESIRE

Desires

I am the whirring of the world
unappeased sway between here and elsewhere
mute foliage of cactus
coarse wood that conceals the gecko
rays of the yellow chameleon sky
bed for the world-book
whose pages are so many waves of the quest
for ever begun again

Caress

stars are glazed dates
that punctuate jet-black sky
a vulva waits for the kiss of the wind

and the faded coat of last night
runs after its beautiful shadow

Truce

I scatter my voice all over the town
there water outlines time
I mingle my body with fragrances
rising from night
there I drown my distress
I search in your eyes for our quarrels from long ago
defeated clans weaving the canvas of strife
I ask the succulent plants to return
my tender memory

unsure you listen to the whir
of my cracks
postpone till tomorrow
the night's approach

Untitled

I tickle the silence on memory's strands
an angel above my shoulder peeks
at my silky book
and
words hide in the pages' folds
fearing that I might shake out sheets
by the white window sash
and amorous secrets
might fly away in a single wingbeat
my moistened tongue
delighting the nadir of leaf
where my semen is dying in silence
suddenly old

POSTCARDS

The Elixir of Exile

is going to Carthage
to help understand Djibouti
is the elsewhere saving the here
and now for happy days ahead
while waiting for time's salve
on scar-scalds of space

Landmark

facing the foothills of death and life
the wind doesn't breathe a word
humanity shrinks for many confined
to the clan
and the legacy still passed from father to son
immortality wish that binds

After the Rain

and I smelt this city washed by torrential rains
this flea-market town with its present-day stench

and I saw these children's heads,
small black pebbles in puddles of mud

Ambouli River, victorious Acheron,☆ swept everything away
in mighty rage

and Balbala☆☆ slips back into solitude
remains of a past that's not so old

Acacia

prince of the landscape
on your dome a goat moves
slender

a thick cloud of ants caresses your roots
while the goat nibbles your loveliest leaves
the ants shelter themselves from the sun

A Sky Chart

I stir the spoon in the cup
and drink a liquid cloudless sky
dilated time shows its scars
a frieze of water and blooms

day dawns quick as a wave of a hand
God's hand or manna from skies?

Coral Riffs

madreporic reefs
are reports
from sea and omniscient sun

Lament of the Lame Herdsman

with my skinny legs
I've crossed vast desert sands
with my short strides
I've kept up with my camels' pace
so why should I care
if my shrew of a wife slanders my name!

ABDOURAHMAN A. WABERI

Infancy

native land of insouciance
birthplace of ignorance
bulimic for stars

There

I live several leagues
from memory's inland port
old silenced structure
slashed by claws of weather and time

ABDOURAHMAN A. WABERI

Bilal

family altar where Bilal sits enthroned
region's first son
to issue the clarion call from so far away

his stentorian voice descends
against the tide
of history's jewellery box

Anatomy (She-camel)

so easy to kiss
pendulous lip
two-times-two pairs of teeth standing guard
in front of a gullet's trap door

By Night☆

incredible silence, except for the drone of the fridge—
metallic cricket
the pencil's fine tip, its minuscule sex
leaves tracks in the white page's sands, obliging
mistress. The lead spreads scribbles, loves
with a feverish love while the man flings
there his pressing desires—
after-midnight seed.

Japanese Cherry Tree

flowers are showering down
petals of blood blended with milk
the breadfruit tree in the garden bed
reawakens our fondest memories
and in peace
spins its everyday wool

Eight Faces
(inspired by black-and-white photographs)

1

see how Africa smiles though devalued
degraded   deprived
of all there was in her insides
all she had to nourish her children
dispersed from now on
to every shore of the vast world

2

tiny eyes that suddenly turn
the balance of the world
upside down in a blink
gaze not yet old enough to be snuffed

3

here is the rural migrant who seems
to have lost his brother
town's nomad
criss-crossing districts

4

some are left sitting here to watch
time pass them by
others dust themselves off
get up and walk   erect   towards the west
course set for a mirage.

5

remain fearlessly in one's own space
escape the greedy camera's eye
watch the sky
the hourglass of time has sped up
the shipwreck of old age at hand

6

photograph someone's core
with the weight of their smile
memory and history guessed at
flickering now
and again in eyes

7

face adorned with a thin smile
something to make your way through a crowd
sometimes hostile sometimes kind
a thin smile
a calmness hard-won
by countering blows from destiny's cleated soles

8

he doesn't appear to be lost in time
and persists in smiling at us
handsome and strong
black and young
with gusto he'll feast
on the yam of life

Yesterday's Tales

the feminine lips of the tiger orchid
have nothing to hide
pitch-black night   everything sleeps   even silence
the bones of the past are here   visible in evening streets

laurels weep for their Daphne
Apollo is off chasing skirts in Abyssinia

go, drop anchor further away
leave the Eritrean Sea
for better skies

the bard equipped with a sword tells you
my land is poor   there is nothing for sale
black gold, rare wood, azure pearls?
nothing but wind   migratory winds—
mirages of water and dreams of herds

confidence in ourselves
evaporates like morning dew
sucked up by the eye of the sun

black often
pink from time to time

how far we've come from saying yes to abducting the coffin

TOMBEAU

Shattered Vision ☆

Child's smile. Watercolour of white teeth.
Simple beauty with unrouged lips. Not a post-
card. Little girls before you with
wide eyes beg for bread. Laughs suppressed
like a pair of sobs.

Grieving Dawn

for Tahar Djaout✩–
may his whiskers blossom beyond time

dawn drapes its velvet mantle of ash grey
on my days
and I weep over Tahar Djaout
killers sharpen their cutlasses stained with blood
they seize me by the neck
I am thrown face-down into the dirt
drums separate keys of the drunken night
they drag me by the hair
I drink my own sap and join the nameless dead

Elegy for a Fly

à Sony Labou Tansi☆

a little pious fly was flitting about in the empty space
of my mind—pale purple she was
with her headlight eyes one would have said a bush taxi
wilting along a bumpy way

subdued by the khamsin's scorching blast
she came to land on my chapped lips
wrought by thirst and frenzied course
through meanders of memory lapse

gravel and black stones
such is the landscape's essence!

one thousand torments later the fly succumbed
sans murmurs
so too a poet the following year

Ai-yai-yai

the eye drinks, doesn't merely see
the eye grows quicker than the finger
achieves negative exploits
and even positive ones, agreed!
the eye perceives all around the hand of God
like silk the eye caresses things
man dies seated
upright or stretched out on earth hands crossed
feet in front and body stiff
life steals away like a thief

Dharma

o young man weep your fill
disoriented like the star torn apart
without sun nor teeming reef
your eye seeks its Orient before you
your consciousness: borrowed coat worn thin

WHITE THREAD BLACK THREAD

there are days filled with air
boots of wind
clicking on pavement of Rue Saint-Martin

days of boredom with arrogant lips
I welcome my fears in massive groves

there are azure days
gathering the dazzling marbles of childhood
an entire life in the echo of my tongue

there are people of no account
whose names never figure in any log

there are days
when we sigh
I miss your shadow
in order to voice
the beloved's absence

there are days when we must be there
in weather good or foul

where my face is pure
as if just emerged from the fountain of youth
a star makes light of my dizzy spell
a lizard rushes to language's low wall

there are days when it feels so good
to walk on our native soil
between fig trees and loose stones
cactus and rock
dust and earth

so long as we can tell apart

a white thread from black
to feed the whirlwind of fire
of dawns that come again

ROSARY FOR TIMBUKTU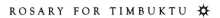

a small amphora full of water
for ritual ablutions

in hollows of arid valleys
in delight when a day begins

in the rustling and budding of time
I have nothing that's mine—except the fear of God

God is the one who provides for the life
He gave me
until the ultimate hour
when night shall cease to be

like a butterfly in the night
who jumps
with joy
into fire

where stars shine
opposite us

Allah
Al·lah
A——llah
two open syllables
repeated over and over again
a name
usher of lives

Allah
Al·lah
A——llah
to get your head out of sleep is a chore
if the soul isn't seeking light
and waging wars inside your own self

Arif
the one who knows
grandeur his cloak
his thirst without bounds
a mustard seed
his pride

from Cheikna
the lesson is drawn
he said
humble yourself and you shall appear
like the full moon
whose image is only seen
reflected in water

don't be
boastful like smoke
which ascends to the sky
while only a product
of earth

ABDOURAHMAN A. WABERI

the dog of my deepest self
is there
curled on the ground
in front of the kennel of life
naked
like a newborn
waiting for us to attend to his needs

NOTES

p. 5

Ardoukoba: Name of a young volcano in the Republic of Djibouti.

p. 6

Habash: Ethiopia.

Bilal: Of Abyssinian descent and a former slave, Bilal, Islam's first muezzin, was one of the faithful companions of Prophet Muhammad.

p. 13

Oum Kalthoum: Oum Kalthoum, who died in 1975, was known as *Kawkab al-Sharq* ('Star of the East'), and is considered the greatest Arabic female vocalist. [Trans.]

p. 15

we'll have to make room for the banished 'p': The sound 'p' does not exist in the Somali language. [Trans.]

p. 16

muslin damask cashmere gazelle alcove: All the words in the second and third lines of the first stanza, as well as 'azure', have Arabic roots. [Trans.]

p. 18

Ouabain: Historically, strophanthus seeds were used as a source of arrow poison. The abbreviation 'n.f.' stands for a feminine noun. [Trans.]

p. 19

Mazisi Kunene: From 'Return of the Golden Age' in *The Ancestors and the Sacred Mountain*, (London: Heinemann, 1982). Mazisi Kunene, a South African poet born in 1930, wrote in Zulu and then translated himself into English.

p. 21

Edmond Jabès: Edmond Jabès (1912–91), an Egyptian Jew, was a writer and poet, known for his elliptical style. Forced into exile after the Suez crisis, he fled to Paris where he eventually received numerous accolades, including France's Grand National Prize for Poetry. [Trans.]

p. 26

eye-opener: This eye-opener, implicitly carrying an underground root stolen from Somali, could be Dawn, sister to the horizon.

p. 33

Panurge: A character invented by the sixteenth-century French novelist, Rabelais. In one story, Panurge, angry at being overcharged for a sheep, throws the sheep into the sea. [Trans.]

p. 25

Qamis: An Arabic word referring to a long shirt or tunic worn in traditional dress. [Trans.]

p. 47

'*Vicious Acheron*': The Acheron, in Greek mythology, was a river in Hades. 'Victorious Acheron' alludes to a poem about loss written by Gerard de Nerval. [Trans.]

Balbala: Balbala used to be a shantytown in Djibouti. Today it is a poor city susceptible to devastating flash floods.

p. 56

By Night: In a fortuitous coincidence, 'pencil' and 'penis' in English are derived from the same Latin root. [Trans.]

p. 65

Shattered Vision: Title borrowed from Rabah Belamri (1946–95), blind Algerian writer.

p. 66

Tahar Djaout: Tahar Djaout (1965–93) was a prize-winning Algerian journalist, poet and fiction writer murdered by an Islamic extremist group. [Trans.]

p. 67

Sony Labou Tansi: Sony Labou Tansi (1947–95) was a prize-winning African dramatist, novelist, theatre director and actor. He is considered to be one of the finest francophone African writers. [Trans.]

p. 71

'White Thread, Black Thread': The title of this poem refers to a quotation from the Koran. [Trans.]

p. 77

'A Rosary for Timbuktu': This prayer, consisting of six poems, is dedicated to the treasure of Timbuktu, destroyed by Islamic extremists. [Trans.]